Dating For Men

Alpha Male Strategies, Social Skills To Create A Relationship, Online Dating Tips And Effortlessly Attract More Women

Edwin Dray

The information herein is provided for educational purposes exclusively and is universal. The presentation of the data is without contractual agreement or any kind of warranty assurance.

All trademarks inside this book are for clarifying purposes only and are possessed by the owners themselves, not allied with this document.

Disclaimer

All erudition supplied in this book are specified for educational and academic purpose only. The author is not in any way in charge of any outcomes that emerge from utilizing this book. Constructive efforts have been made to render information that is both precise and effective; however, the author is not to be held answerable for the accuracy or use/misuse of this information.

Foreword

I will like to thank you for taking the very first step of trusting me and deciding to purchase/read this life-transforming book. Thanks for investing your time and resources on this product.

I can assure you of precise outcomes if you will diligently follow the specific blueprint I lay bare in the information handbook you are currently checking out. It has transformed lives, and I firmly believe it will equally change your own life too.

All the information I provided in this Do It Yourself piece is easy to absorb and practice.

INTRODUCTION

First of all, thank you for making an effort to get this book. This book is a concentration of everything I've found out and used to become successful. Not just that, but the information shared in the book is a selection of practical things that have been used to train other men to become very productive with dating.

As you embark on your journey towards self-improvement as a man, assume that the knowledge you gain from this book works till tested otherwise.

This book lays it on the line for you regarding what women find appealing in a man and shows you step-by-step how you can not just act in appealing ways only but also become an attractive man. And when you become a handsome man, you'll attain your dreams just by being yourself.

A personal note to those of you who may be thinking: "Yeah, sounds great, but I am who I am, and that isn't changing." Bullshit. Change is in your mind. As you picture, so you will be. Ninety percent of being successful thinks you can be successful. We're talking about the psychological picture here, which is a strategy that nearly all leading athletes use. They envision themselves achieving success.

Think of this for a moment: let's pretend you just won the lottery game, won big. You've got a million dollars. If you were to stroll into a club tonight, do you believe you'd walk more confidently?

Project yourself with more authority? Sure, you would! Girls often understand when a man's got something, be it money, power, or anything, just by the way he manages himself.

And I'm going to show you not just how to manage yourself, but how to truly be more confident, so that your walk and talk almost yell to the world, "Hey, I am confident!".

Women have somehow evolved to be instinctively and intensely drawn to strong and dominant alpha males-- not wussy, weak "nice guys.".

Unfortunately, very few men are born natural alpha males. Most of the alpha males out there are self-made, learning to develop within themselves the fundamental traits that make alpha males the amazing, effective, positively intimidating men that they are.

The primary aim of this book is to equip you with the tools you require and the qualities you need to develop in order to become an alpha male having fantastic success with the dating game. Dive right in, get started, and find the crucial traits you need to become an alpha male.

CHAPTER ONE

Where do I take her to on the first date, and what can I do to make a great impression?

That very first date is special and is something that many women will ruminate upon and ponder as lots of women take much enjoyment from this time of being wooed and getting romantic attention. This is the reason why men might feel under pressure to get it. Trying to get it right can be a battle for some low self-esteem guys, especially attempting to consider somewhere unique to take her or what to plan. Many will suggest a sumptuous meal, which can work quite well as it provides a focus. Food can give a subject of conversation, specifically if the woman takes pleasure in cooking, eating, or baking out. Going out for a meal does involve lengthy conversations, and some low self-esteem guys may have a hard time with this and may prefer just to meet for a fast drink or coffee.

If continuing a chat is difficult or concern, then an excellent option may be to go to the movie theatre or to listen to a band or orchestra as this will limit the communication and offer a common interest to discuss in the interval or when the program has finished.

If, though, the couple have met through a dating website and have not seen each other before, it may be much better to keep the meeting quick, if this is the case perhaps meeting for a couple of drinks or a coffee would be safer and permit the chance to make a rash retreat.

Having a shared interest works well in relationships and is a fantastic way for couples to meet. I have worked with some men who discover some voice tones or accents, particularly irritating. If this were the case, then it would be meaningless to pursue a relationship with the individual. Having said this, for some guys talking on the telephone is not always a simple option, and I have worked with some men who have a real worry of using the phone and find it hard to sound confident and articulate.

If a male turns up on a date looking neglected, with foul breath or body smell, it is not likely he will see her for a 2nd date if this is the very best he can do to impress her. Providing time and factors to consider to looks and health is essential. It is also a great idea not to consume anything ahead of time that is going to duplicate and result in the lady being showered with offending burps. Halitosis is a significant turn off for a lot of individuals, and women do appear to revel in good smells, so if a male uses aftershave or deodorant, it can go a long way.

Whatever the couple decides to do on the first date, the man must remember that many women do delight in a little love. It can be the basic things the man does that will offer the female a long-lasting and great impression of their date and will go far in making her feel both feminine and special. The guy could make an effort to open the door for the lady, bring her some flowers, compliment her appearance; he might be the one to go to the bar for beverages or merely stroll on the outside of the pavement. At the end of the night, he could provide to walk her to her car, bus stop, or house. If she is on her way home, try sending a text to guarantee she got home securely. This will all be noted and remembered by her. These little gestures can make so much distinction to how the female will feel, both about herself and her date.

The Worst First Date Mistakes Guys Make

When you are setting up to go out with someone, you need to prevent making mistakes. With the website modern age, you are going to have the ability to see what the worst first date mistakes people make are, and how to avoid them. Although you could search online for the worst first date mistakes people make, you will find that numerous women will affirm the reality that men still make errors. There are a couple of things that you can do to ensure that you're not anywhere near the issue areas if you desire to prevent making any errors. With that in mind, the following tips will use in almost any circumstance.

- Program Up Late

The very first thing that you need to advise yourself about is straightforward, be on time. In truth, don't merely be on time, be early. Amidst the worst very first date errors people make, time is everything. Don't' be late, and search the location before the date. In fact, go to the place where you're going to meet your date and walk, look at some signals, and see what to anticipate. You are going to be able to eliminate a bit of the nerve that usually comes with first dates if you do this.

- Focus on her only

You shouldn't be browsing in front of her. Check out her eyes, and let her be your world. Do not under any situations take a look around for other women, even if there are gorgeous girls all around. You have to stay focused. You need to flirt with her, speak with her, listen, and take notice of the words that are coming out of her mouth. Do not attempt to alter subjects, try to stay within her viewpoint, and do whatever it takes to avoid the worst first date errors people make. If you can't do this, then you're not ready to date on a major level.

- Make Her Pay

The biggest problem that a lot of women have on very first dates is that their partner does not pay for things. You ought to be all set to pay for things. Rather, you must pay for her supper, coffee, or easy aspects. Making her pay is the wrong concept. Instead, focus on spending for the date.

Do not spend the very first date discussing your special interests.

What should I talk about on the very first date?

What to talk about on the very first date is typically a significant concern for many men. Small talk and Asperger syndrome do not go well together, and for someone with AS initiating and maintaining irrelevant social chit chat is nearly impossible. It requires a lot of ideas and effort on their part.

The majority of women will desire to feel that the guy has an interest in them and is pleased with her appearance. They will anticipate him to be able to make them feel good, and an excellent way to start is by using a compliment about how she looks. The guy may compliment her hair, her smile, her fragrance, or what she is wearing. To have a couple of rehearsed compliments can be helpful and certainly assist break the ice when you first meet. Be careful about making comments that are too personal or sexual at this early phase in dating as this could be translated as sexual thoughts, which for some will feel too forward or threatening. Remarking that she has generous boobs or a voluptuous bottom is not likely to be well gotten at this stage.

There is a general rule of topics to prevent at this early stage in the courtship unless it is currently understood that both individuals share the same opinion as each other. These are:

- Politics
- Religion
- Morality
- Sex
- How to discipline children

- Women chauffeurs
- Her look, weight, or gown sense (unless complimentary).
- Third World.
- Capital penalty.
- Mental health.
- Physical health.
- His unique interest (unless it is shared or she expresses an interest in it).
- If his ex

At the end of the evening, it is always rewarding to attempt to complete on a welcome note, which can quickly be attained by him stating how much he has taken pleasure in the night, the conversation, and the business. If the man has chosen, he wants to see the woman again, then he can state so. It is best not to anticipate that the female will desire to organize it with him there and then. It is merely a way of letting her know he is delighted to see her once again. However, he wants to let her call him when she is free. By doing this, she will not feel under pressure and will value him offering her time to think about. She may well want to arrange another date there and then, which will feel great; however, if she does not do this and neither does she make contact, then the man needs to leave it there and not pester her with texts and calls.

How do I know when or if to take it further?

In my research, I asked females to explain what attracted them to their partners, and the details that came back generally shared the very same thread throughout. Lots specified that they felt the guy they are contented with is a complete gentleman; they explained him as gentle, kind, peaceful, well mannered, attentive, and having other favorable qualities, all of which they recognized early on in their very first meeting. The women were very taken by the men that valued them and did not put pressure on them to be physically intimate.

So how can a guy learn what she desires? One method to inspect out if she wants more than a platonic relationship with him is for him to touch her in a way that is friendly and not sexual and see how she reacts. For instance, if they have gone out for a meal and her hands are on the table, he may attempt resting his hand by hers and see if she moves her hand closer or if she rapidly pulls her hand away. Then the male may gently take her hand and hold it in his if she does not pull away. When they are walking together, the guy might use his arm to link or ask if he may hold her hand. Asking authorization is always the safest method, but for some men, their worry of rejection is so intense that they discover they can not ask the question. What if the woman says no? If this is the case, it might feel much safer to use texting or emailing to ask if she would like more from the relationship or not.

Texting or emailing has been a lifesaver for some men, and using this form of communication has felt much safer for them. An ideal time to text is typically after a date, saying something like:

' Hello Mary. You looked absolutely beautiful tonight; it was challenging for me not to kiss you! Love John x'.

Once this is sent, he will need to wait to see what she sends outback. The female might text, stating she is not prepared for that or does not feel that way. If she does, then it is significant that he had discovered before he did try to take it even more and found himself in an uneasy and challenging scenario. Or she just might say:' Thank you, John. Yes, I wish you had kissed me! '.

How can I know when or if to take it even more?

If it is the latter, then he has his response, and next time the couple meets up, he may wish to try a mild kiss at the end of the date.

You may have discovered I USED the wording 'gentle kiss' how a person kisses are essential for most women and also often seen as indicating what type of enthusiast the guy will be. The very first kiss is something that the lady will remember and replay in her mind. This is an essential relocation, and it is another part of dating that the guy requires to attempt to get right; it can practically be seen as the crossroads that will take the dating into an intimate relationship or end it dead in its tracks.

Kissing should be respectful and romantic; it must be soft, gentle, and focused. For some women, there is absolutely nothing worse than being kissed in a manner that might leave them feeling as though their mouths have been powerfully raped! There is absolutely nothing worse than being kissed by someone who is intrusive with their tongue or covers the woman's mouth with their saliva. These are significant turn-offs and will signal to the female that if this is how the male kisses, then this is how he will treat her in bed.

Another rule is for the man not to translate a kiss as a free license to begin touching the lady's breasts, bottom, or vagina. The man may stroke the non-erogenous places of her body such as her back, arms or her hair but that should be as far as he takes it at this phase unless she makes it extremely obvious by offering a clear physical or spoken sign that she would like more from him, for example, if she touches the guy's penis or verbally asks him to touch her. Even then, it would still be worth him checking it out by asking her the question.

After the kiss, it would make her feel great if he complimented her, such as informing her he has wanted to kiss her, considering that he first met her or that she is gorgeous. It is the small things he does that she will keep in mind at this phase. For him to show her regard while letting her understand, he finds her a very desirable female will all belong to the journey into the next phase, the sexual stage.

When again the signs a woman gives off that she is drawn into a male can be very subtle and not easy to read; the factor for this is that the woman does not want to get it incorrect either. Many women still hold on to the notion that it is for the man to initiate or to make the first repositioning and will frequently likewise hold the belief that he will have read her non-verbal signals that it is OK to make a relocation, such as hold her hand or kiss her.

The best place to meet a prospective partner?

The task of finding a prospective partner can seem overwhelming for the guy with low self-esteem. To cover every possible avenue would be difficult as relationships can grow out of the most unlikely situations and encounters. I have selected the most likely locations and the most accessible. Everybody will have a choice, and what will match one person might not suit another-- it will be for the reader to choose what might work best for them. Four of the most common locations are highlighted alongside their advantages and disadvantages.

The night club

This way of meeting girls is rarely effective for some men. The majority will find night clubs traumatic due to the possibility of sensory overload, triggered by the loud music, flashing lights, crowded bars, and dance floors, which all tend to form a big portion of the night club scene. When faced with the distraction of so much background sound, sensory overload can feel extremely overwhelming, and some men have actually reported finding it difficult to hold a discussion. If the guy wants to interact with a woman he is trying to develop a connection with, this can feel quite difficult.

However, on the other hand, some men may find such location as a bonus as they can use the loud noise as a reason to avoid little talk and long discussions. This eases the pressure of having to consider what to say, and they can simply enjoy the dancing.

For the majority of men, however, there is a propensity to avoid night clubs, and this could be due to a history of disappointments. There have been accounts of men being set up by women to make their partners jealous, or just being used to buy drinks. It is recommended that if the club is a choice being considered, you should go there with a group or with a good friend who can be depended on for suggestions or to spot the caution signs. Sadly this is not often possible for some men, and they can end up feeling both overwhelmed and confused by the whole experience.

If a woman approaches a man in a club, he has to ask himself: Why? He needs to assure himself she is not with another man and merely trying to make that man generous. If unsure, he should ask her if she is with her partner. If she asks for a drink in the very first few sentences, it would be reasonable to be cautious as it is likely she is using him just to get complimentary drinks. Nevertheless, asking her if she would like a drink, giving her a compliment, or dancing within her proximity can be ways of first approaching a lady in a club. If the lady declines the drink, overlooks the compliment, or goes far from his space on the dance floor, this implies she is not interested, and he should not pursue it.

If he is still with the woman at the end of the night, then he could suggest he wants to see her once again or ask if she would like to exchange mobile numbers to correspond. Then he must wish her well and make his way home if she says she would rather leave it for now. But if she says it would be good to see him once again or concurs to him giving her a lift home, he needs not to assume this means she desires sex. Unless she makes it very clear by saying so and asking if he wishes to have sex with her, the man must never assume that sex is on the program. Often bear in mind that as alcohol can promote an incorrect complacency, it can also trigger an absence of control. The man needs not to put himself at risk or become a danger to anyone else.

Pros:

- It is most likely to provide the opportunity of a one night stand if that is what you are trying to find.
- If you like dancing), - You get to dance
- It is much easier to lose yourself in the crowd.
- You will not be expected to talk much.

- There will be the opportunity to meet women of different backgrounds, cultures, and ages.

Cons:

- It is not perfect for finding a significant or long-lasting partner.
- It can cause sensory overload.
- Too much alcohol can trigger a wrong complacency and loss of control.
- There is a risk of someone reacting violently.

- There is a risk of being used to purchase drugs, drinks, or cigarettes.
- It can be restricted to a younger age.

Workplace

A large proportion of couples meet within a work environment. It does, nevertheless, need knowledge of what the company rules are, as some workplaces do not endure relationships within the workforce. To disregard this might result in one or both of the couples needing to leave their place of employment, and for many people, this would be both stressful and troublesome. The repercussion of this is most likely to have a negative effect on the relationship that has been recently developed.

Assuming the company does not prohibit relationships between personnel, the office can be a way of meeting a potential partner. Obviously, the kind of work a person does will make a difference to this, as some jobs can be male-controlled, such as engineering or IT. If, on the other hand, the work environment provides a combined climate and there is a lady that the man is attracted to, then the workplace can offer a perfect opportunity to learn more about somebody. It will provide both the opportunity to get to know each other gradually and to develop a connection before embarking on the possibility of a relationship. This all sounds extremely straightforward; the concern is that some men can not inform whether a lady is, in fact, attracted to them, or if she is merely enjoying their relationship and wants no more.

Starting a work-related relationship is, in some cases, left to gatherings such as the Christmas party, as this can achieve two things: (1) the guy can see if she features a partner, which would dismiss the possibility of taking it further, and (2) if she is alone, he can see if she looks out his company. If the Christmas party is not an alternative and as long as she is not using a wedding or engagement ring, then the man will need to do a little investigation to discover whether she is readily available. This could be achieved by asking someone who knows her if she has a partner and even asking her directly.

This needs tact, and the male should tread carefully so as to avoid intruding upon her level of sensitivities or to make himself susceptible to being rejected. One way forward might be to learn if any new restaurant has opened in the vicinity and then mention this and ask her whether she has been there or heard any reports about it. If she has a partner, this will give her the chance to let the man know, by saying that she went there with her boyfriend or is planning to choose him. Most women will be honest and make a potential pursuer to see if they are with someone, although this might not always be the case. If the man is on Facebook, he could ask her if she has a Facebook account, and if so, he might request to add her as a friend on Facebook-- this is likely to inform him of her relationship status.

If a man has found a lady in his work environment who he is attracted to, he will need to be cautious about how he approaches the possibility of a date with her. If she informs him she is with somebody or overlooks his efforts to strike up a conversation; then he should withdraw. If not, he might find himself the target of ridicule or, even worse, being reported for harassment.

Having stated that, work-based relationships are often effective, and couples have met this way. If the relationship is unsuccessful, the work environment can end up being a source of tension or distress, making it challenging for one or both to continue working there. If the man finds himself the target of destructive gossip, this can be made worse. All he can do is to put on a brave face, disregard the chatter and understand that these things quickly blow over, so long as he does not react.

Pros

- There might be a typical denominator between you.

- There might be time to construct up a relationship.

- If she is in a relationship already, - There might be the ability to check out.

- Work social events are a good time to meet someone.

- Relationships formed by doing this are typically successful.

Cons:

- Relationships might be restricted as part of the business's policy.

- It can be tough to determine if the female has a partner.

- It can be difficult to be sure whether her interest is romantic or simply platonic.

The job of discovering a potential partner can appear frustrating for the male with AS, and I am typically asked the best way to achieve this. If a female approaches a man in a club, he requires to ask himself: Why? He needs to assure himself she is not with another guy and merely attempting to make that man envious. Unless she makes it extremely clear by stating so and asking if he desires to have sex with her, the male needs never ever to presume that sex is on the program. If the man is on Facebook, he could likewise ask her if she has a Facebook account and if so, he might request to include her on his friend list.

The man could end up being talkative if he gets it wrong or reveals excessive information. But if the relationship ends, then it can make the work environment stressful.

Social Or Unique Interest Groups

A search on the internet might indicate that there is a social group for single grownups running in the local vicinity. Social groups are run by a particular set of individuals who interact, putting together a program of activities to hook up with new friends via the social platform. Members of the group then choose which occasions they would like to go to or take part in.

The cost of signing up with these groups can vary, and this will require to be inspected thoroughly. In addition, the age variety of the group will also need to be examined, as some groups can be for younger grownups in their twenties and thirties, whereas others will be for older age.

Social groups can be a terrific way to be familiar with others without the pressures of needing to try to form a relationship. Many will not be in a relationship and will just be searching for business and friends that they can hang out with, so be sure of the type of social group you are joining.

Numerous platforms offer a wide variety of activities and interests to select from, such as strolling, dancing, dining, theatre, and weekends away. They give the member the choice to engage as much as they like and to reoccur as they please.

As social groups, there are also interest groups such as the Ramblers (www.ramblers.org.uk), hill-walking groups, photography groups, and numerous others. These interest-specific groups can be perfect for a man if he has a particular interest, as he will have the ability to share this with others along with the social side of the group. A considerable benefit of meeting somebody in an interest group is that they will be someone who shares the same interest, and this will give both an excellent beginning point in developing a relationship.

Pros

- It will indicate there is someone to satisfy you.
- There is no pressure to have a relationship.
- You will have the ability to get to understand someone initially.
- There are lots of various venues and activities.
- You can discover somebody who shares your interests.

Cons

- You may not proceed with everybody in the group.
- Some groups are costly to charge or sign up with to join in the activities.
- Being part of a group might be effort and quite strenuous for you.

Dating Websites

Internet dating for numerous guys might appear to be an ideal choice as it offers the chance to select a woman beforehand they discover attractive from her photo and who seems to share their interests.

Being able to organize the first meeting is another significant bonus in using dating sites, and I have understood some guys go to excellent lengths to attempt to get this right. Let me share a story of a man that fixes a dinner where he had set up to meet his date the following night. He discovered a good place to park his automobile and inspected what change he may require for the parking meter, and he timed the length of time it took him to arrive by car and after that by foot to the dining establishment.

He selected a location for them to sit in and picked which seating position he preferred for himself, which in this case was to have his back against the wall. He studied the menu, chose what he would eat and how much it would cost, took down where is the toilet, and were about the white wines. By doing this, he reduced the worry part he suffered from unforeseeable issues on the night. When he went on to have his date, he was more relaxed and felt more positive than he would have. I am delighted to state that they went on to a 2nd date.

Website dating can allow the man to feel more in control than he would in a random situation; however, it mustn't become a way of life and a habit. Internet dating for some guys can become a fascination, which can be the failure of a relationship that could have worked. In some men, their capability to read other individuals' motives and covert agendas are complicated. This will often make them unable to tell whether someone is sly or friendly. This challenge in checking out others' intentions can make them vulnerable to exploitation when dating, especially to financial exploitation. This can make him a prime target for being taken off the expenses. If a guy discovers himself continually spending in a relationship, then he requires to draw back from being overgenerous and see what reaction this causes from the lady. If a female is authentic, then she will understand, compromise and arrangement will be made.

I have also encountered clients who have talked of women on dating websites from foreign countries who were very keen on marital relationships. It has later transpired that the women's primary intention for the relationship was to get to a brand-new house or car. Obviously, there is no other way he can be sure if her motives are real till they are together as a couple, but it might assist if he visits her in her place or if he introduces her to his family and friends to seek their opinion.

Nevertheless, after a while, when the relationship becomes more down to earth, and the enthusiasm subsides, he might feel dissatisfied and, after that, decide that she is wrong for him, that she deceived him. He might then decide that he has still not found the right female and begin the search all over again. I have understood this pattern to continue for several years for some guys until, eventually, they meet the right one.

Pros

- There is the opportunity to select someone who appears ideal.
- There is access to women from other cultures or nations.
- There is a chance to build a relationship using e-mail instead of needing to make a conversation.
- It is possible to have constructed a relationship with the first conference.
- A place and time for the meeting can be chosen.
- It enables the choice of inspecting the location ahead of time.

Cons

- You might not always get replies to your emails.
- Emails might not lead to a date.
- A date may not turn up.
- The person you meet may not look the very same as their photo.
- You might be set up for monetary gain or other benefits.

- If there is any chemistry between you. Until you meet the person, you will not understand.
- Internet dating can become a fixation.

How do I understand if she is drawn into me?
Never assume that her sensations are the very same as yours, and the tourist attraction is mutual.

If it is the first encounter and a woman is drawn into a man, she will look into his eyes, and she will likewise smile just a fleeting smile, and after that, she will look away. As long as he smiles back, she will watch again and smile. If they are already in communication, the man may discover that she leans her body towards him and maybe makes physical contact with him in conversation. For instance, she might affectionately touch his arm while talking. What do these natural gestures signal for a man?

The world of dating and all the complexities it brings can seem like a headache for guys, as it includes having the ability to read the other person's body language, facial expressions, and voice articulation. These are all things men will find extremely difficult to do. A female may be quite mindful of avoiding appearing over-keen in the early stages of the meeting as she may fear rejection.

Trouble in reading the social hints provided by others will cause an issue for man in getting the timing right in the dating game, as it will not come naturally for him. This can be made harder by the possibility that there might currently be a history of him being rejected by his peers and found out understanding that he can sometimes misread other individuals. This alone could significantly weaken his self-confidence in understanding whether he is getting the pacing.

The man will now remain in the scenario that he has discovered a lady he likes brought, but he is now left with no idea of whether his sensations and desires are reciprocated; moreover, if they are on a romantic or relationship level. If the female has vocalized her feelings, then this will not be a problem, but this is highly unlikely, as she may likewise fear rejection or the danger of being implicated of being too forward.

Determining whether the attraction is reciprocated can put some men through absolute torment, sometimes affecting both their health and frame of mind

Often problems can develop from the guy making the presumption that if he likes a lady, then she must feel the same about him, and the tourist attraction is shared. This is often not the case, and it is necessary that this is never ever presumed unless the female has definitely spelled out her sensations of destination to him. The reason this misassumption can occur is a lack of theory of the mind and not having the ability to see the circumstance from the other individual's viewpoint. The only frame of mind the man will be conscious of will be his sensations, and these feelings of attraction might be powerful. The strength of his impressions might be exaggerated due to his passion for finding a girlfriend, and it is this that may trigger him to presume that the lady shares his destination and feels as highly as he does.

This misreading can likewise happen in reverse, and I discover some clients can hold the belief that others are thinking adversely about them, simply by seeing another person's look or a look. They will miss the fact that a female is flirting with them or finds them appealing. The presumption might be wrong, and this is why it is essential to check out just what the lady feels before any action is taken. It is very important not to get too carried away by feelings of attraction to a specific female or to assume she feels the very same, as you may be too forward. The lady may feel men as being egotistical or arrogant, and his chances of charming her will be lost.

When a female is giving signals that she is drawn into a guy, she will keep eye contact a couple of seconds longer than would usually take place. Eye contact can be robust for some men to make, and they will have a problem with making or maintaining eye contact, particularly when in communication.

One of the reasons for this is that they might discover it tough to focus on what they or the other is saying if they are attempting to keep eye contact or read another individual's eye contact. I have actually discovered some will go to fantastic lengths to attempt to enhance this skill by going to neuro-linguistic shows (NLP) courses, checking out body language books, or just from observation of soaps and films.

I have noted some of the signs to look for that might show that a female is interested, or not, as the case may be.

Eye Contact

Interested

- She takes longer than usual eye contact.
- She averts and looks back rather rapidly.

Not interested

- She may avert.
- She might look down but offer brief darting glances.

Mouth

Interested

- She smiles; this can be minor.
- She sulks.

Not interested

- She does not smile at all.
- She will just smile at you in a welcoming or if you say something amusing.
- She will provide an extremely tight-lipped smile, which may suggest she is annoyed or worried.

Distance

Interested

- If sitting by you or in front of you, she will lean towards you.
- She will enable you to come into her area, or she will enter yours and stand or sit, preferably near you.
- Her arms will be open and welcoming.

Not interested

- She will lean away from you.
- She will ensure that there is no physical touch between you.
- She will keep her arms folded.

Touch

Interested

- She may make physical contact with you; this might be a pat, rubbing your arm, permitting her foot or knee to make contact with you.
- She might give a hug when bidding farewell or greeting you.

Not interested

- She will pull away from any physical contact.
- Her greetings and farewells will be quick and short, with no effort to touch you.

Body Movements

Interested

- She might keep having fun with her hair or pressing it back.
- Her arms are open.
- Her feet are pointed towards you.
- She maintains eye contact.

Not interested

- Her arms are folded.
- She averts.
- She looks past you.
- She points her feet far from you.

Interaction

Interested

- She asks concerns.
- She gives compliments.
- She chuckles with you (not at you).

Not interested

- She offers short one-syllable responses.
- She sighs.
- She does not ask you questions.

This list is not sure-fire, as it can not take into account a female's character; she may be shy and therefore feel nervous and show a closed body movement. On the other hand, some women are demonstrative and extremely tactile, and although they will appear friendly, they will not be flirting at all. It should likewise be taken into consideration whether a female has been drinking alcohol, as this will decrease her inhibitions, making her more likely to show flirty or affectionate behavior indiscriminately, if the man can ask someone else's viewpoint this would be useful. If this is not possible, then he may consider informing her in a text that he likes her and will quickly find by her reply if his feelings are reciprocated. He should appreciate this and not try to take it any further if the female feels the same, then that will be fantastic; if she does not.

She is unlikely to be offended by understanding he likes her. However, if he pursues her and does not respect her feelings, she will be offended, and he will get harass.

At the ripe aging of 23, a friend of mine got his very first girlfriend. Even though he was simply a law student, barely getting by, he continued to invest over thousands of dollars on the girl is simply one brief, whirlwind of a month, blowing through expensive wines at restaurants and other unnecessary presents. My pal was sad for months later, not to point out that he had to get a part-time task to renew his bank account.

Been there, done that. I've bought girls suppers, motion pictures even a $500 ring that I saved up for back in high school. It used to be that I 'd routinely bring a girl a $30 arrangement of flowers on our first date.

All I 'd desired out of the deal was to get laid. It appeared a fundamental deal the chick would get the stuff I purchased for her, and in exchange, all she needs to do is spread her legs.

Sound familiar? Are you annoyed when you don't get laid like you should, after all the cash you've invested?

Well, here are the essential things: you're running on a false assumption. Money invested doesn't always equal legs opening.

The problem with lavishing cash on a lady who hasn't accepted, communicate a negative message to her.

I understand that saying "do not buy things for ladies" Men are brought up to think that if there's something of worth that we desire, we require to be ready to shell out what it takes to buy it? Well, when it comes to inanimate items that don't believe on their own, that's real.

Here are some of the errors.

- Revealing off Your Cash

This is continuously a typical error most men make during dating. Usually, men like to reveal ladies they have the money even on the first date. This can be extremely hazardous. An accountable lady searching for the right guy may neglect your cash. To date effectively as a guy, you have to be very simple and charming. Keep the woman in the dark up until you come nearer to her.

- Being Arrogant

Numerous men appear to be strong-headed when they head out to date. Sure, men can be bossy because it is innate in them. There's always the need to mellow down when you desire to satisfy a woman. You have to indulge a lady and reveal her just how much you care as you date her. You can't attain this if you're too strong-headed and bossy.

- Excess Talking without listening

Some men talk too much when they go out for a date. For the most part, such men will continuously keep talking about their achievements in life. They find it tough to give their partners enough area to talk. When their partners are talking, they also discover it difficult to listen. This can be very dangerous. A dating relationship is a two-way thing. You have to offer the other individual sufficient room to talk. When dating a girl, you require to give her modification to air her views. When she's talking, you likewise have to listen to her.

- Speaking about an ex while staying with the new date.

Many men make this mistake. They keep speaking about their unsightly experience with their ex sweethearts as they meet their new dates. This can be appalling. When you're dating a brand-new girl, there's no point going over about your ex. If you keep doing that, you can quickly put her off. You suppose to focus on how to keep the brand-new woman pleased as you consult with her on a regular basis.

- Demanding for sex prematurely

Many men likewise make this mistake! They quickly ask sex, even at the preliminary stages of the relationship. You need to avoid this if you truly wish to enjoy dating a girl. A cheap woman can quickly fall to your sex demand; however, this may be the beginning of problems in the relationship.

Avoid the habits below, and you'll instantly separate yourself above 95% of the other men out there. That by itself, when women notice it, right away makes them feel wetter around you.

1. Bragging

" You must see my amazing home."

" I'm about to get a raise approximately six figures a year!" "I have a huge cock."

High self-confidence is attractive to women. Think highly of yourself, and a female will think extremely of you.

It's alright to make an obvious joke about putting yourself down(said with a playful tone of voice)

Frequently, men do make typical dating mistakes. If you're a guy interested in dating, there's a need for you to understand more about the standard errors and how to avoid them.

2. Putting other individuals down

And because women are delicate creatures who sympathize with the less lucky. Don't put down people who are your sexual competitors, because that too reveals your insecurity. Instead just don't take note of them, since they're not worthwhile of your attention.

Never make a big offer out of it when you do purchase the female things. Say something like, "I'll pay for the coffee. It's no big deal." What that states to her is that you're more interested in the social interaction that the two of you are having, which you barely believe about the beverage you just bought her.

It also means that there are no strings attached. By stating, "it's no huge deal," you make it clear that you're not putting pressure on her to reciprocate what you've provided for her.

" Buying me things since he wants something later" is a behavior that numerous women think about manipulative and results in the male being denied sex. And to be rather honest, lots of men fall right into that trap by making a big production out of purchasing the woman nice things. Don't be that guy.

The main thing you require to do is to realize why you're doing something.

Never purchase things for a female or do favors for her because you believe you need to make her approval. Instead, adopt the frame of mind of the dominant male: anything you provide for her is conditional on her having earned it.

Tips For Success in Online Dating for Men.

Women do receive a lot of offers, but many of them fall under one of a selected variety of categories. If you are sending a girl an e-mail, and it falls under among the following classifications, she will most likely delete it and move on.

I understand that this may seem unreasonable - after all, you put in the time to compose to her, so definitely she owes you the common decency of composing back?

Again, incorrect.

If a lady is especially appealing, it's not uncommon for her to receive 50 or perhaps 100 brand-new e-mails every day. She simply does not have time to go through each one and reply. So she needs to produce psychologically faster ways that separate the wheat from the chaff. She will scroll down her list of e-mails, declining most without even opening them, just stopping to open the ones that stimulate her interest in some method.

Here are six typical mistakes that you can prevent that will set you ahead of the competitors.

1. Having no subject line, or a dull subject line in your initial e-mail to her.

Many people just put 'hi' in the subject line of the email. Believe about what happens when she logs on and sees 50 new emails; all showed in a list. All she can see is your username and the subject line of your email. If 49 of the e-mails say 'hi' as the subject line, and one e-mail has a different subject, which is probably to catch her attention? So think of how to make yourself stand apart from the crowd.

2. Sending out overtly sexual preliminary emails.

This ought to be a no brainer, but considering that numerous guys are doing it, it requires a reference. If you send her an overtly sexual first e-mail, she will think 'pervert,' delete you and probably block you at the same time. Yes, women indeed enjoy sex as much as men, including filthy talk; however, there is a location and a time. What kind of reaction would you expect if you strolled up to her on the street and began spewing a lot of filth talk at her? You get the same response online - other than you simply don't get to see the action. You simply get deleted.

3. Sending an uninteresting first email.

A lot of very first e-mails from men fall under this classification. Example: 'Hey there, my name is John, and I read your profile and liked the appearance of you. I see you like cooking and tennis. I like cooking and tennis too, so I feel we have something in common. Inspect my profile and compose back if you like what you see.'.

I assure you - if she's been on the dating website for any length of time, she has read that same e-mail 100 times. It's the very same problem as number 1) on this list - you are not separating yourself from the crowd. You are not creating a spark of excitement in her brain that makes her wish to strike the reply button.

4. Not having an excellent set of images in your profile.

Typically she will read your very first email, and presuming you have created some kind of interest within her, she will open up your profile. What does she see recalling at her? A single, rough cam taken photo that appears like you're locked away in your bedroom someplace. Does that give the image of a social, fun guy who has lots of pals and is fun to be around? Nope. So you require to get out with friends in numerous social settings (not only bars) and get some great images taken that appear like you are having a good time. It will make all the difference in terms of the impression.

5. Having a profile filled with spelling mistakes or 'txt spk.'

Unless you're 12 years old, 'txt spk' is not cool. So compose in full sentences, at least provide the impression and attempt that you went to school. And there's no reason for being sloppy and having a profile loaded with spelling errors. In the back of her mind, she will be believing 'if he makes this little effort on his dating profile, how much effort does he took into the rest of his life?' Not a great start.

6. Having a boring profile.

Comparable to the boring very first e-mail, the uninteresting profile is the most common issue that most people have. Essentially their profile details a list of hobbies 'I like fishing, football, reading, tennis, climbing up, the movies, nights in and nights out. Email me if you like the same.' Absolutely nothing exciting there. You need to attempt and paint a photo with your words. Get her picturing the situation in her mind and explain it in brilliant detail. When she reads it, she will envision herself there with you, which is the initial step to her belonging to your life.

So it may take you half an hour to spruce up your profile. And you might require to take a few minutes to read her profile in future and think about an intriguing or amusing e-mail to send her that ignites her curiosity enough to think 'I want to learn more about this man' and hit the reply button.

Trust me that additional time will be well invested when you have your pick of stunning charms eager to snaffle you up and make you their man.

Error 1: Using bad pictures.

The Internet has ended up being a place full of fraudsters who develop dating profiles just to fulfill women and ask them for money if you have not already realized by now. These fraudsters generally only have one image in their profile; hence it is the norm for the majority of knowledgeable individuals who date online to believe that one picture profiles do not show the real individual. So start publishing several images of yourself, particularly ones where you are enjoying yourself together with your friends to reveal that you have a correct social life.

Error 2: Being impolite or nasty.

When she does not reply to your e-mail right away due to your frustration, in some cases, it is tempting to send a lady a nasty e-mail. However, you have got to keep your mood under check. Simply send one polite follow-up email if she doesn't respond and after that proceed. You have got to understand that attractive women get hit on a lot online, and they receive lots of e-mails daily.

Error 3: Not reading any profiles.

If you haven't realized it by now, most women dislike getting emails that are basic and do not discuss anything about their profile. Although it might take a while at the start because you need to go through their profiles and after that send a lot of emails with comments related to their profiles, it is worth it at the end.

Error 4: Being interested too quickly.

A lot of men are brought in by appearances, and frequently they simply discover a profile they choose and like that they like the female or are interested in the lady currently. This is probably a grave mistake to make as you don't know anything about her life at all, and for you, all understand she may have posted phony photos or pushed her profile. Instead, use online dating sites to meet lady offline to get to understand more about her.

Error 5: 'Dating' online.

Although there is no doubt that online dating websites are a terrific place to satisfy women, they are most likely one of the worst places to construct a relationship. You ought to attempt to get her phone number as soon as possible and arrange a meet-up offline as soon as you meet or discover somebody you are interested in. Don't waste your time dating online as you never know whether the person behind that profile is real or just out to bring you for a ride.

CHAPTER FOUR

Are you Mr.Nice Guy?

I'm going to try to describe precisely why a lady is not going to wish to end up with a Mr. Nice.

Unless she is totally out of alternatives, hopeless, and somewhat desperate. Then I think it's safe to say that she might not be that much of a quality lady after all, if this is the case. In any occasion, here are the reasons why good people are more turned down, discarded, and cheated on by the women who are in their ideal minds:

1. Nice Guys Have Difficulty Doing the RIGHT Thing.

Yeah, you heard me. Great guys have a great deal of trouble doing what is right in a specific scenario. Instead of doing what's right, good guys tend to decide for there a lot easier path and choose to do what is nice. If you can't do the best thing, then that suggests you make choices based upon trying to keep everybody else happy rather than making sure that you'll enjoy it yourself.

Since this will make you a pushover to her and anyone else, a female who has her actions together will not tolerate this. She'll see you as the type of man that is easily led by others and who is incapable of taking the required actions to makes things right in any given situation.

If you are a good person that does the great thing instead of the ideal thing, she'll merely see you as being unreliable. She'll realize that you won't have the ability to manage the disputes of life, which you will not have the ability to show individual stability.

2. Being Mr. Nice Guy Makes You Seem Less Authentic.

As a man, it's essential to be as authentic as possible in the choices that you make. It's just a part of being a fully grown guy. Great guys tend to have a problem with credibility because they will state "yes" to any request that comes their way.

Good people likewise have a difficult time sorting through the massive amounts of demands upon their time and resources.

In other words, nice people allow a lot of unnecessary commitments in their lives. Their lives are merely filled with excessive "fluff." They deal with other people's concerns, other individual needs, and other individuals' plans. Great people place themselves second to everything and everyone else, and that makes typically them a disposing ground for others.

You can be assured that no female is going to want a male who is a discarding ground for somebody else. If you can't be real to yourself, a female will simply feel as if you will not be true to her. She will not be able to feel secure with you, and thus her capability to become intimate with you will be incredibly limited, if at all possible.

3. Nice Guys Give Their Power Away to Women.

You've probably been allowing women (mom, sister, partner, girlfriend, etc.) to make the most critical choices of your life, and even the not-so essential ones as well. You've probably established a sort of relationship with women where you need to have them enjoy with you for you to be delighted with yourself. And think me; you don't wish to be in this type of situation.

Why? Well, if a female sense that you quickly offer your power away to her, she might recognize that you might do it for another woman. She'll question what makes her so unique anyhow.

What she wants is a guy in control of himself, and at times, her too. Providing your power away to a female just suggests that you offer her the approval to authorize you, which you've given her the enjoyment of ensuring that your requirements are always fulfilled.

This is a no-no.

No woman in her best mind wants a man to provide his power away to her. She will feel pushed into the position of being the "man in charge," and she will not like it. She dislikes it. And even worse, she hates men who make her feel that method.

Why Nice Guys Never Win With Women.
Remember, how no female in her right mind would wish to be with Mr. Nice-Guy? Well, fortunately for Mr. Nice-Guy, we have lots of women out there who are not entirely in their ideal minds at all. Because he can still put other people's requirements before his and keep a relationship with a lady, this is fantastic for our friend Mr. Nice-Guy. However, what sort of lady will he attract or perhaps create precisely?

Well, since of the way good people treat people, they tend to bring in numerous types of women that might prey upon their gullible, ignorant, and excessively kind-hearted ways. Even worse, they end up creating women like this as they end up being passive in their relationships. They might attract women with all sorts of problems, whatever from mentally clingy women to gold-diggers. You 'd be surprised at the kinds of women that good people naturally attract without even recognizing it.

There is an old cliché that says that there is somebody out there for everyone. I think its kind of real considering that a nice man and his manipulative methods can discover some measure of what he feels is joy in a relationship with a similarly manipulative female that truly desires to control the relationship or control. No man in his best mind would want to be in a relationship with a damaged and manipulative lady.

Don't get me wrong here; I understand that nobody is perfect and that everybody is going to have their problems in a relationship, however that does not suggest that you must go out trying to find the worst of the bunch since you do have the choice to avoid it.

A nice guy may attract a very possessive lady that will put high needs on his time and resources. Being the nice person that he is, he'll discover to bear with her high demands to keep her pleased thinking that he's doing the right thing when in fact, he's merely doing the great thing. At the same time, he's suffering within, getting fed up, and internally contravened attempting to please this woman and trying to keep himself pleased and sane.

This guy is suffering because of his lack of individual borders. The more he neglects her habits and accepts it as something that he needs to deal with, the more he will suffer internally and begin to do not like the female and even worsen himself. No lady can appreciate him if he can not respect himself. The great man may soon find out that without self-regard, he can never discover true happiness in a relationship with his ideal woman.

In brief, a top-quality woman likes and wants a guy that has a high sense of pride. It is a necessity.

Man, who considers himself 'high-quality,' needs to be with a female who understands how to respect his limits. Anything less will be unfulfilling, unsatisfying, and entirely unsustainable to him.

10 Things You Should Know About the Nice Guy.
So before I reveal you how to tackle eliminating your Mr. Nice-Guy personality, let's see exactly just how much of these nice man beliefs and behaviors you are struggling with. Here are ten things you MUST understand about the Nice Guy:

1. A nice person believes that if he is excellent, offering, and caring, he will get joy, love, and satisfaction from others in return. He plays a sort of game with himself thinking that he deserves to be dealt with a particular method because of his niceness.

2. The nice guy offers to do things for a lady he barely knows. He has a strong desire to get the approval of women. This can be any female, specifically the ones that he discovers appealing and deserving of his excess amounts of niceness.

3. The nice guy avoids disputes by keeping his opinions or may even end up being reasonable with a woman when he does not actually concur. This nice person tends to think that in order to keep the peace and preserve the love and appreciation from a lady, he must concur with her at all expense. If it costs him his self-regard, he does this even.

4. The nice guy tries to take and fix the care of all her problems. He is drawn to attempting to help a lady out in any method that he possibly can. This is one of the primary reasons a nice person tends to bring in a lot of damaged women. His desire to be her Mr. Fix-It makes him vulnerable to fall into relationships with problematic women.

5. The nice guy has an overwhelming need to seek approval from other people. It's the type of approval looking for, whereas he might feel guilty for stating "no" to somebody, or he may end up

being uneasy with himself when he's disrespectful, even if it's out of necessity.

6. The nice person attempts to conceal his perceived flaws and mistakes from others. Due to the fact that he wants everyone's approval and he wishes to be seen in the finest light possible, he's ready to go to extreme lengths to make himself look as flawless as humanly possible. He's manipulative to the third degree.

7. The nice guy is always searching for the proper way to do things rather than simply making an effort at something. The nice guy is afraid of stopping working and, of course, making a mistake in front of others. He does not desire to step on anyone's toes. Because he does not want to rock the boat, he 'd rather not do anything if he does not have all the responses. Sadly, his fear of failure and criticism culminates in meaningless perfectionism and continuous procrastination. He not does anything and accomplishes less than nothing.

8. The nice guy tends to over-analyze everything instead of feeling things out for himself. In some cases, the nice person can be a bit of a perfectionist, and preferably of just going with the

circulation and just letting things occur, he 'd rather have whatever planned and represented in his own best universe.

9. The nice guy has trouble making his needs a concern. Instead, he 'd rather pretend that what he wants.

Isn't that important and that he's a team gamer. Or he'll believe that by putting his requirements on the back burner he's one hell of a man which everybody ought to always bear in mind that he's such an excellent man which everybody needs to like him.

10. The nice guy is quite often mentally dependent on his woman. He's so reliant on his lady for his psychological wellness that he'll go through terrific lengths to guarantee that his woman's needs are satisfied before his and that he always gets her approval. Since in the end, he thinks that as long as she's delighted, he's happy.

Why You Must Kill the Nice Guy Inside.

When life presses you around, do you press back or push your back and take it? Do you linger believing to yourself that individuals should treat you better and that things should always go your method, or do you get out of your convenience zone and expand your circle of influence? Are you confident enough to go out and attempt, and sometimes stop working, to get your requirements satisfied or do you sit by the wayside waiting for the scraps of life and love to be given out to you? What have you done recently to expand your capacity for problem-solving and managing disputes?

Well, if a woman senses that you quickly give your power away to her, she may recognize that you may do it for another female. They may draw in women with all sorts of issues, whatever from mentally needy women to gold-diggers.

Depending upon how honest and simple you are with yourself while addressing those concerns, it might be time for you to KILL your Mr. Nice Guy Have no fear; I'm here to assist you through the process since I've learned how to murder my own Mr. Nice Guy consistently whenever he chooses to appear. Yes, it will make you uncomfortable, but that's just the point. Do not worry; I'll walk you through it.

The thing you ought to do is to learn the traits of a good man and end up being utterly mindful of when you or some other guy is acting like one. Find out to end up being mindful of your behavior, as this is the initial step to changing the ineffective way you react to people, specifically women.

The second action is to become honest with yourself and analyze yourself to see which of the good guy qualities apply to you the most. It's unlikely that you're a complete pushover when it comes to your relationships, as most good people tend to be at different points on the right guy scale. Figure out which habits are nearly automatic to you and catch yourself in the act.

As you interact with individuals, specifically women, take notice of yourself and what you state and do to prevent disputes and fight. See yourself in the act of doing the good thing instead of the ideal thing and start to choose the harder path consciously. It will make you a much better guy.

Instead of taking a great way out, challenge yourself purposely. Make an effort to get out there and get your requirements met.

Keep in mind to use common sense in this regard. You're not attempting to be disagreeable for disagreeing sake. If you disagree, you need to have a valid point to make, or if you're asserting yourself, then you ought to be attempting to get your needs satisfied without infringing upon the rights and wellness of others. Do not be embarrassed to request what you desire or to have a firm opinion about something.

Always take a look at the chance as a possibility to develop your self-esteem and assert yourself. If you consider it as a discipline or a practice, you'll be comfortable when you fail from time to time. But on the other hand, you'll also realize that with each mindful effort, you're getting much more powerful as a man. Always bear in mind that the practice of frustrating individuals to be authentic with yourself and others will strengthen your borders.

And even though the thought of individuals not liking you might tempt you to take the right way out, just keep in mind that most of the time, when you do defend yourself and act assertively in your relationships, individuals will appreciate you. You will get self-confidence in the long run.

- Stop Living for a Woman's Approval.

If you're presently living for a woman's approval, you're probably not one of the happiest people around. Every day that passes and you seek a woman's support, a little bit of your inner manliness passes away. You end up with a deep-rooted feeling of powerlessness and suffering, and you're too contrasted with doing anything about it. Or possibly, you're just unaware of what's going on inside of you.

As a man, you were indicated to be self-reliant, independent, and extremely capable of leading yourself and your family in the best way you perhaps can. When you go about your life seeking the approval of women, you end up losing these qualities. You wind up providing up your rights as a male, and for that reason, you'll find your life heading in a direction you never meant it to.

How to Stop Seeking a Woman's Approval by Becoming Comfortable with "NO."

The most valuable thing you can do for yourself right now as a fully grown male who wishes to become a much better guy for the lady you want is this: Become comfortable telling people "NO," and hearing "NO" from others.

Truthfully, if you followed simply this one piece of suggestions, you my pal are on your method to a much happier and productive life not only with women but also in every other relationship.

No is a fantastic word. It's a great thing. And yes, I know we live in a world that promotes stating yes to life and having a favorable psychological mindset, but stating no to others, to yourself, and hearing no and becoming comfy with it will make you feel a lot more powerful and in control of your life.

Learning to be comfy will assist you to overcome the concept of requiring the approval from other individuals. It's most likely the fastest method to become a more fully grown, confident, and self-assured man. You'll discover how to focus on win-win solutions in your relationships, and your ability to influence others will increase exponentially.

Make no error; the only way you can help others is if you are devoid of their approval. It's impossible to assist someone if you require them to like you authentically. You can't have both. So discover to become extremely comfy with people NOT liking you. Among the very best ways to do this is to end up being a no-man yourself.

Why Telling Her "NO" Makes Her Happy.

An intellectual woman is much more drawn into a guy who knows what he is and wants determined to get it. She admires and respects a man who follows his inner convictions regardless of what others may think. When she needs to hear it, she'll happily follow a guy who can inform her no.

A lady, understanding that she can sometimes be an emotional and unreasonable creature, will unconsciously desire a man and desire who can put her in her location when the time comes. Since it implies that you show courage and stability in sticking to your inner convictions, it's essential to her survival and to that of her offspring.

She'll understand that you appreciate yourself initially and foremost and that you're more than going to assert yourself and stand your ground if you feel as if your needs aren't being met or if your limits are being imposed upon. If you can defend yourself, she'll understand that you can defend her as well.

The more self-respect she sees that you have for the satisfaction of your requirements, she'll also understand that you'll be more than capable of satisfying her own. For her to see this quality, you should REFUSE to be a doormat for other people, including her, by asserting yourself. If you desire to become the kind of guy that can both attract and keep a high-quality lady in your life, timidity will get you nowhere. You need to have guts and iron nuts to say NO.

The second step is to become fully honest with yourself and analyze yourself to see which of the excellent person qualities apply to you the many. It's not likely that you're a total pushover when it comes to your relationships, as many good guys tend to be at various points on the good guy scale. Knowing When to Say "No" to NO and "Yes" to YES

When you discover a female that you're interested in, and you're getting to understand her a bit more in a dating relationship, think of saying no as a way to qualify her for higher access to more of you.

Do not merely offer her everything she requests for at the start. The word no ought to be used to communicate your limits, which you just let individuals have access to more of you (your intellect, your time, your social circle, your feelings, and so on) when you discover them reasonable to your values and standards.

When to say no and when to say yes, as you develop a meaningful relationship with a woman, it's essential to understand. It's all about balance and understanding the significance of being clear about what you will or will not tolerate from others. To become intimate with another individual, you need to want to compromise and jeopardize.

Constantly keep in mind that such things are best done in a relationship that is based on shared regard and commitment between two people.

If you can keep a positive attitude, stick to your weapons, and keep moving forward, every no will help make a much better guy out of you.

CHAPTER FIVE

The Three Kind of Men

The Beta Male, "Nice Guy."

When I was maturing, my mama, aunties, and other older ladies always told me that to get a girlfriend; I would need to be a good man. I 'd require to continuously buy a girl flowers, offer her presents, and take her out to eat.

" Wow," I believed, "I'll require to have a truly great task so I can have all that money to invest!".

Suddenly it prevailed knowledge that to be successful with women, you required to imitate an asshole rather than a good person.

I attempted that advice out and discovered that when I acted like a jerk, some women reacted to me more.

So I took a challenge looking at the men who were successful with women, the ones who weren't, and the ones in between, and I found out that there are three classes of men.

At the bottom of the list are the good guys, who make up most of the male population. The good guy is a guy who generally pleads for sex. He appears at a female's doorstep with flowers, drives her to an expensive restaurant, and buys her filet mignon with great white wine.

And you need to know what's paradoxical here? Think it or not, women consider nice people to be manipulative.

It's quite apparent to the lady why the great person buys her so many things. "They're just after something!" is a common mantra that women duplicate about nice guys. Nevertheless, she thinks he may potentially have excellent relationship potential.

And when sex does come, it's a substantial event, and the woman makes a huge offer about it. Hopefully, the guy does not have a high sex drive, because he won't be able to get sex whenever he desires.

Why don't good people succeed? The problem with the great man is that not just do women consider him manipulative; they also see him as boring. The good man talks about sensible things like diplomacy or how a cars and truck engine runs. In some cases, he boasts about himself and just how much cash he makes, suggesting that he can buy things for the lady. "How lame," she thinks.

Taking part in rational discussion and trying to impress a female with your smarts and earning capacity is a mistake that 99% of men make. Since it interacts neediness and low worth, it kills a female's attraction for you. You would not be trying to impress her if you weren't seeking her approval.

It snaps her out of her trance. So refrain from discussing that short article on Chinese trade policies you read in The Economist until you're socializing with your male buddies.

You need not pretend to be some type of moron around ladies. Women find it attractive when a person is a specialist in something. A guy who's an expert is automatically an alpha male. Simply make sure to mesmerize her with the knowledge you share. Don't bore her.

Women just want to have a good time, as the tune goes, and the good, dull guy isn't enjoyable.

The quickest and most convenient way to eliminate any destination a lady might be starting to feel for you is to feel insecure about yourself, or to be needy, or to seek approval. When you have the frame of mind of being desperate to please, you wind up coming on too strong, too early. You become clingy. It's like you're begging.

The Problem With Being Her "Friend."

Have you ever went for being buddies with a girl orbiting around her as the months' pass, hoping she will eventually succumb to you? Great deals of men do this, particularly the shyer ones.

These men end up functioning as emotional tampons for women. They listen attentively as their female friends inform them about what jerks the real men in their lives are.

Women just merely don't like spineless men for more than good friends. And when you imitate a good person and follow the woman's plan, and accept her to make decisions, she does not respect you.

And that's why the great guy doesn't get laid. Like I stated, women don't like to take obligation for sex. You, as the man, need to take that obligation and lead the method. That's what women desire you to do, and believe me, they love it when you do!

Being overly interested in a female's ideas and feelings is a waste of time because the bottom line is you can't control what a lady believes or feels. You can only control yourself. Rather of taking women too seriously (which offers them power over you, making you needy and unattractive), just see them as conventional sources of enjoyment and satisfaction in your life. That's it.

Next time you're with a woman, attempt to state "no" to her eventually. Saying "no" can be useful for women. Do it in a soft method, like this:

Her: "Let's go see a movie."

You: "No, not now. Let's enter in the next hour."

If she sees you as a difficulty, then she will be excited by you instead of bored.

If you state YES to everything your lady suggests, then she will quickly be saying NO to you, and in the worst place of all, the bedroom.

The alpha male is amazing to women because his happiness comes from within, so he does not burden her with any duty for his psychological state.

Let me state something here: your inner state is essential with women. For them to see you as adorable, you have to love yourself first. You have to have enthusiasm for your life, and you've got to go for what you want.

There are a lot of good guys out there who are down on themselves and insecure. That's why when it comes to love, great men do complete last.

The Jerk

The excellent person makes the fatal mistake of attracting their logic, whereas the one good idea the jerk does is to appeal to a woman's feelings.

Because they get women turned on by being so persistent and then going for the lay, jerks get laid. They are sexually aggressive, unlike the good people who are sexually passive. While the jerk creates unfavorable emotions within women, a minimum of them still creating feelings, rather than the great man who bores women.

Such women often act insecure and weird when it concerns relationships, so they're not the kind of women a well-adjusted male would wish to opt for in any case.

The bright side is that there is a higher level of men yet, whom I call the alpha males, who cause positive feelings within women without any genuine negatives.

The Alpha Male

In society, alpha males are the leaders; individuals look up to them. The alpha male is positive, socially dominant, outgoing, fun, a leader, safe and secure in himself, has high self-confidence, and is a guy who has his shit together.

When a lady states something sarcastic, the beta male gets angered, while the alpha male laughs about it since he understands women resemble his silly little sis. Studies of social scenarios have revealed that dominant people will mark their area in numerous nonverbal ways, such as using up space with their bodies, using a louder voice, controlling conversations, and using strong eye contact. Individuals around the alpha male tend to get sucked into his truth because he's intriguing and makes them feel comfy.

Since he isn't needy, the alpha male doesn't feel possessive or jealous over females. He also does not smother women by putting them up on a pedestal. Because of this, he understands that any female would be fortunate to have him, so if any specific lady doesn't opt for him, then that's her loss, not his.

On the other hand, the beta male fidgets, have low social status, is usually a follower instead of a leader, feels typically privately resentful, has low self-confidence, and is clingy and desperate with women.

I used to be beta. I was depressed and resentful. I desired a girlfriend because I thought having one would make my life worth living.

Six Beta Male Behaviors To Avoid

Here's something you may not understand about us people: we're wired to attach more weight to negative details about somebody than we do to positive details. That's why you can be having a great discussion with someone, and after that, all of a sudden, you change your mind about them.

So, because one wrong move can shoot down 100 great ones, it's crucial to avoid unfavorable habits that are characteristic of low-status males, or betas, if you do not desire women to treat you like crap and lead you on. These beta attributes to prevent are:

1) Seeking approval by ending sentences with, "isn't"? These concerns tacked onto the completion of sentences make you sound weak-willed.

2) Trying to dominate. Instead, just do it. Have a stronger mental reality and mindset than anyone else.

Presume individuals are there to follow you since you are the man.

3) Being belligerent, either with women or with other men.

The alpha male can stay calm under pressure and walk away when he needs to. Beginning a battle is a sign that you're a man with low status. Battling to acquire the affections of a lady is the supreme type of approval seeking, which decreases your attractiveness. With that said, however, if some person violates your limits and starts shit with you (like let's say you get bullied), there are occasions when you need to stand up for yourself.

4) Following the other person's schedule and discussing what they want to talk about, even if you find it boring.The alpha male just discusses what he desires to. Enjoy any alpha male in action (e.g., Politicians and CEOs), and you will observe this phenomenon. When an alpha male is bored, he does not conceal his disinterest. Do not offer individuals your attention until they've earned it.

5) Trying to mislead individuals and show that you're smarter than the individual you're talking with. You discover that the best leaders are safe enough when you look at leaders in business boardrooms or governor's mansions.

6) Checking out every pretty girl you see. A guy who's getting laid left and right doesn't have time for this, so you should not, either. See how they start examining you out and wishing to show themselves to you.

If they are a natural leader, alpha males presume the mantle of leadership as their birthright and act. They don't care much about what others believe. They do their own thing and do not seek approval.

While the jerk develops negative emotions within women, at least they are still producing feelings, as opposed to the great man who tires women.

The alpha male does not feel jealous or possessive over women because he isn't needy. Because of this, he knows that any female would be lucky to have him, so if anyone particular woman doesn't go for him, then that's her loss, not his.

And when you speak with a lady, lead the discussion. Mesmerize her attention.

As you deal with your habits, you will likewise work on adopting the mindset of an alpha male. The first thing I see that all alpha males have in common is that they assume individuals will follow their lead.

Be a catch to all women, Act as if pussy is no big deal to you because it's not a massive offer to men who get laid all the time. Act as if all your manly desires are entirely natural. You have no reason to excuse or conceal your libido the way good people do!

Be positive: Success originates from confidence. Presume you will be successful, and your mindset will increase the odds that you will. Presume that you are tempting to women.

Be brave and effective: At the very same time, be natural and enjoyable. Be a bit of a bad boy; however, don't be a jerk. If you want, have a devilish smile on your face.

Do what you please in life: Be real to your feelings. If you do not desire to do something, then don't. Be truthful with yourself. Be your own man.

CHAPTER SIX

Get Rid of Non-verbal Cues that Scream You Are Non-dominant

What do you think is something that makes a man most appealing to women?

You convey your dominant male status merely by acting the method dominant men do, by knowingly managing the nonverbal cues you send, thus developing the impression within a lady that you are alpha.

This technique is called the association principle. Within the mind of a female, you're associating yourself with desirable manly qualities while dissociating yourself from undesirable "nice guy" qualities.

Similarly, you can use impression management to control what the woman thinks about you.

What's supremacy? It's social power, which originates from assertiveness. As you go through your procedure of self-improvement, eventually, you will internalize the concepts of this book and become an alpha male.

Right now, you're going to discover how to imitate an alpha male, giving the impression of dominance by using your voice, your eyes, your habits, and your posture.

Your eyes are the primary nonverbal cue that tells individuals you're an alpha male. A dominant male is not afraid to gaze straight at individuals. By averting your gaze, you communicate submissiveness. When you look down, you interact with self-consciousness, shame, and a sense of low status.

Research studies have shown that using a soft, peaceful voice can produce the impression that you aren't assertive.

When you speak, attempt to let your words circulate and do not be afraid to speak your mind. People who hedge and hesitate are perceived as less powerful than those who do not.

Enjoy your habits and quirks. Attempt to avoid the following non- spoken indications of beta status:

1) **Using "ah" and "um," partial sentences, and partial words.** Research studies have revealed that individuals think about others who talk like this to do not have self-confidence and not be too brilliant. It's a sign of anxiousness. The factor we say "um" is because we're scared we're going to be interrupted by the other person. Instead, do not be afraid to stop briefly for impact. Stopping briefly previously essential points will make you seem more proficient, and individuals will remember what you say.

2) **Speaking too fast.** This produces the impression that you feel anxious and have low confidence. A regular, comfortable speaking rate differs within a moderate range from 125 to 150 words per minute. Decrease!

3) **Speaking with a monotone voice, also understood as mumbling.** Individuals with a narrow pitch range are deemed unassertive, uninteresting, and not have in self-confidence. So differ your pitch, and you will be viewed as outgoing and alpha.

4) **Pausing too long before responding to a concern**. This shows that you're thinking too hard for your response, which makes you appear indecisive. It likewise looks like you're trying too difficult to win the other individual's approval.

5) **Holding your hands in front of you**. This is a protective gesture. Instead, hold yourself open and vulnerable because you feel no fear.

6) **Twitching your fingers or hands.** When you're throughout the table from someone, there's a natural inclination to have fun with sugar packages or straw wrappers with your fingers. Do not. And don't drum your fingers on the table, women dislike that.

7) **Touching your face when you talk.** This suggests that you believe too hard, you're indecisive, or that you feel shy. To communicate self-confidence, hold your hands together in a steeple shape in front of your chest or face. (A lot of teachers do this when they are lecturing.) When you need a substantial display of self-confidence is holding your hands at your hips, another posture that will help you. Police officers do this.

8) Folding or crossing your arms in front of you. On unusual celebrations, it is possible to fold your arms in an alpha style (watch Brad Pitt in the movie Fight Club for a great demonstration of this), however as a general rule, avoid it.

9) Rigid or stooped posture. An alpha male has a relaxed posture, whether he's standing or sitting. Relax and expanded.

10) Looking down. The alpha male holds his head high. It reveals enthusiasm. Looking down at the flooring telegraphs "loser." Keep your chin up. Expose your neck-- don't worry, no one's going to choke you! Take a look at the individual you're speaking with; remember what I stated about utilizing your eyes.

11) Nervous facial gestures such as lip licking, pursing your lips, jerking your nose, and biting your lips. An alpha male has an unwinded face and mouth because he fears nobody.

12) Excessive smiling. Studies of primates have revealed that beta males will smile as a method to signify their harmlessness to more powerful males. Beta human beings smile to reveal they're not a threat.

13) Walking quickly as part of your regular walk. Rather, walk a little slower than typical, nearly as if you're swaggering. You're alpha-- no one's chasing you, and you're not rushing to please anyone else. If you're not in a rush to get someplace, walk like you're unwinded and positive. Think: "I am the male. I can make any woman delighted.".

14) Walking just with your legs. Don't hesitate to move your torso and arms. Attempt this: walk as if you 'd simply had massive success and felt on top of the world. Enjoy what you do with your body. You might discover yourself moving your arms together with your shoulders and having a minor bounce in your step. Now, do that all the time.

15) **Slouching**. You do not have to stand annoyingly ramrod straight, but you need to have your shoulders back.

1) **Blinking a lot**. Slightly blink your eyes slowly. Do not close your eyes in discomfort. Simply let your eyelids unwind. In reality, let them sag a bit. Do not be bug-eyed.

17) **Moving your eyes back and forth when you speak.** That's extremely beta. Look at the other individual's face when you're in a discussion, and you're doing the talking.

18) **Holding too much eye contact when the other person speaks.** Non-stop eye contact makes you look needy, socially slowed down, and, honestly, like a weirdo. Rather let your eyes blur and after that gazed at her eyes. Look through her rather than at her. From extensive screening, I've discovered that looking at a lady about two-thirds of the time is optimum. By the way, just hold the gaze when she's telling you something genuinely intriguing. Otherwise, concentrate on other things like her breasts, her hair, things going on around you, etc.

19) **Being uneasy with your eyes.** The bottom line is that your eyes ought to be comfortable, relaxed, assertive, and sexual.

20) **Looking down or to the side before answering a female's question**. Look up to the team if you do require to look away before responding to think. Studies have revealed that this shows more confidence.

21) **Being afraid to touch a female, and thus being non-touching**. Be positive about it when you feel women-- any anxiousness at all can be fatal for your relations with her.. Be gentle if you use extreme pressure, you reveal your insecurity. (Since you're alpha, obviously she will follow you, so there's no requirement to be anything besides spirited and tender.)

22) **Turning your head quickly when someone desires your attention**. Instead, use the movements that you would when you're at mouse sluggish and relaxed. You're not at anybody's beck and call. You're alpha, remember?

23) **Using long, convoluted sentences**. Alphas keep it brief and to the point.

Don't feel bad if you inevitably slip up and utilize some of these nonverbal cues from time to time. No one's best, so don't beat yourself up about it, especially when you're talking with a female. Let it go and keep the discussion moving.

When you consider such things too much while talking, you begin to question yourself, and when that happens, you feel insecure and distressed and become reluctant. Instead, just deal with staying nonchalant yet genuine at all times.

It's adequate to simply understand how you interact non-verbally with everything you do, since knowing ways you will start to avoid unfavorable communications far more.

Nine Nonverbal Cues That Say, "I'm Likable."

I've currently listed non-verbals that convey dominance. There are some great overlap deals of those signals, such as sustained eye looking while you speak that communicate supremacy likewise makes you more likable. Often dominance signals (such as leaning back) can make you more distant.

Be conscious of the following quiet strategies that magnetically get a girl to you:

1) Lean forward when you're sitting throughout from someone who is informing you something. This communicates interest in what they are stating. It's crucial to make sure that the female is highly interested in you before doing this, given that leaning back is a way for you to play "hard to get non-verbally." Lean

forward to offer the impression that you're easy to talk to when she's interested in you.

2) Directly orient your body and face towards her. Note that you should have supremacy established before doing this, because you lose supremacy by being more direct with your body language.

3) Smile.

4) Have a relaxed and spread-out posture.

5) Dress similarly to your group, but simply a bit cooler than everybody else. If you meet the gown expectations of individuals you engage with, you will be much better liked.

6) Wear lighter-colored and more informal clothes. (However, such clothes likewise interferes with your viewed dominance.).

7) Maintain shared eye contact, go on and look into her eyes, and she will like you. Do not do it more than 70% of the time, though, as stated previously.

8) Make sure your speaking voice is enjoyable, expressive, unwinded, and interested in what is being discussed.

9) Do away with any facial expressions that are not pleasant, an absence of gestures, looking elsewhere, closed body movement, and an uncomfortable-looking posture.

Once again, make sure to strike a balance between dominance and likeability. If you never smile, then the female won't like you. However, if you smile excessively, it makes you appear like you have low social status, you're trying too hard.

Some things, such as an unwinded, spread-out posture, help you with supremacy and likeability, so you should be spread out and relaxed all the time. Your eyes are the number one nonverbal hint that informs individuals you're an alpha male.

CHAPTER SEVEN

Women Want Men That Other Women Want.

Women enjoy men that other women are into. This phenomenon is called preselection. You know how a man strolls into a club with a female on each arm and, all of an unexpected, every other girl is considering him.

And no, this isn't a case of mistaking correlation for causation. Studies have found the same thing: Women are intuitively drawn into men that other women want.

Get a picture of a man, show it to some women, and the women might or may not be drawn into him. Program the same man with a stunning female (or women) and all of an abrupt; he is quickly viewed to be 10X more appealing.

On a final note, this only works if attractive women preselect you. Having some fat uggo chasing after you will have just the opposite result.

When women know that other attractive women desire you, you become 10X more beautiful in their eyes. Now, let's take an appearance in ways you can apply this to your own life.

How To Use The Power Of Preselection.

You may not (yet) be able to take the common alpha male technique of appearing to constantly have a few hot women with you, or strolling around with women hanging off your arms, but that doesn't indicate you can't effectively use the power of preselection to your benefit.

Here are a couple of easy methods you can get going utilizing the power of preselection.

• Post images of yourself with some adorable girls onFacebook. 'Nuff stated.

• Date more women. Remember, dating is not unique. You can date as lots of women at the same time as you like. So date lots of women-- it'll increase your attractiveness in their eyes. You can also integrate this idea with the next one,

• Be vague about your relationship status. If a girl asks, do not state you're single, simply say something like, "It's complicated," and say no more. You might likewise make things even murkier and more mystical by using words such as "girl" and "girlfriend" interchangeably.

• Don't expose your notch count. If a woman asks you how lots of women you've been with, just say something like, "What, today? Few ..." or "If I told you, I 'd have to eliminate you.".

• And more! So get creative.

Nice guys love to invest as much time, effort, and money into women as they possibly can. They incorrectly assume that the more they invest in a woman, the more attraction she feels for them. A bad young boy spends just enough for a woman to rationalize being with him. When you eliminate your inner-nice man's excessive eagerness to please others (especially women), you'll discover individuals (specifically women) progressively seeking your attention and eager to please you.

A man's physical attractiveness plays a far smaller sized function in a woman's attraction than a lady's physical appearance does for us people.

Be Exciting, Mysterious, and Unpredictable
We humans naturally have a minor inferiority complex. You see a hot girl, and you imagine her as the most fantastic, remarkable person ever to live. You picture her living a crazy, amazing life. You feel insufficient by comparison.

In reality, though, hot chicks live very typically, uninteresting lives, similar to the rest of us. That hot chick you felt frightened by? She is most of the time, very bored. She lives a boring, regular, mundane life.

And just as we men frequently view hot women as being too awesome for us (even when they're quite uninteresting and common), so too do women. Women do this to a far, far greater level. That's why women are intensely drawn into dark, strange men. They build up this great fantasy in their mind, something that no truth might ever wish to match.

This is likewise why frequently the very best sex you have with a girl is the very first time you bang her; she's trying her best to please this mysterious alpha guy. However, as you become increasingly more familiar, and she starts to understand increasingly more about you and recognizes that you don't have any other options (i.e., other women wanting to bang you), the sex becomes plain. Dull. Common. She puts less effort into it and desires to have sex less regularly. She goes from eagerly trying to please you to "just tolerating" you. Eventually, you wind up in a sexless marital relationship, and, if you're fortunate and she doesn't have a "headache" for the twelfth night in a row, you may get enthusiastic, once-a-month starfish sex.

This never occurs to alpha males. They (whether consciously or automatically) realize the power of maintaining an air of mystery and unpredictability. They understand that girls regularly forecast an aura of mystery around men that they know really little about. Moreover, they assume the very best.

Don't spill the beans. Do not inform her everything about you, be unclear, cultivate an air of mystery, and let her complete the spaces with her creativity. Be a mystery, man.

The Power Of "Busy."

Do you think high-value alpha males have time to relax with some chick all day? No, of course not. They've got better things to do.

You see, for a lot of 'good guys' make the mistake of assuming that if only they were better if just they could invest more time with a chick, text her more, speak to her more, and go on more shopping journeys with her, then she would be brought in to him. Sadly, not so.

Stay busy. That which is limited is important. If you spend too much time with her, she will inevitably take you for granted.

Crucial Ideas.

1. Tell her less about yourself. Let her fill out the spaces with her imagination. Looking for to impress her only leaves her not impressed, and you discover as needy as if seeking validation or attempting to compensate for a perceived inadequacy as if you feel you're unsatisfactory for her.

2. Spend less time with her. That which is scarce is valuable. Investing every extra minute with her and continuously flooding her with messages ends only in her not valuing you and taking you for granted.

3. Be unpredictable. The unpredictable is amazing and launches dopamine (the brain's satisfaction chemical). Being completely unpredictable, mesmerizes women even more than merely being a dull old foreseeable Joe Blow. Shake things up!

Tease Her.

For example, if a girl asks a great man if she looks fat in a dress, he'll desperately inform her no, that she looks fantastic and gorgeous. If a girl asks an alpha male if she looks fat in a gown, he'll react to it as the dumb concern it is, telling her it appears like she just gained 400 pounds and must take that dress off right away together with her panties and then provide her a wink.

He's not her shoulder to sob on nor her psychological tampon. He's not there to put her at ease and inform her how "fantastic" she is. An alpha male is there to have enjoyable and entertain himself, nothing more, absolutely nothing less.

Don't hesitate to (playfully) give women shit and tease them, especially if they ask/say something downright dumb (e.g., "Do I look fat in this?"). Don't put women on a pedestal. Simply treat them like the typical, boring, farting, pooping individuals they are. Above all, entertain yourself and have a good time.

When you put a woman on a pedestal, all she can do is look down on you. This is a mistake that so numerous people make. They attempt to be so good, do good things for her, go out of their way to impress her, and prioritize her joy above their own.

As if she is the higher-value person, and you're simply some low-value man attempting to offset your inability by being additional significant and continuously looking to impress her and win her approval.

When an alpha male just treats her like a normal person or, in some cases, as if he is the higher-value one, as if he is the prize-- by teasing her, playfully poking enjoyable at her, tinkering her and ruffling her feathers, he discovers as being much greater worth. The lady will look to impress him and win his approval rather than look down on this poor 'good guy' attempting so difficult to win her love.

Here is the major difference between alpha males and good men (likewise referred to as beta males) when it comes to women: A beta male imitate she is the prize. An alpha male acts like he is the prize.

And guess what? Women are hypergamous. Women never want to be the reward. They desire him to be the reward. That's why you hear women discussing how Mr. [X] is "a real catch." Women are biologically hardwired to be brought into men that they feel transcend to them.

Put her on a pedestal, go out of your method to impress, and constantly flex over in reverse for her, and she'll see you as an unattractive, inferior male. Treat her like a normal individual (or take it an action further and imitate you're the remarkable one) by playfully teasing her and providing her a great ribbing from time to time. She'll see you as an attractive, exceptional male. As if you're the reward, not her. And that's what she desires.

Women Love Ambitious Men.

Alpha males do not do this. They have more crucial things to do, whether it be building a service, pursuing an enthusiasm, or founding an empire. They live interesting, daring lives by themselves terms. If they like, they may permit a lady to tag along for the trip, but women are just a device to live, not life itself.

Discover something that thrills or even consumes you, an objective, a greater purpose, an enormous objective-- and aggressively pursue it.

Women don't desire to be your life; they want to belong to it. They want to tag along with a guy as he sets about living an interesting, adventurous life. They do not wish to be the center of his life, his primary focus. Alpha males deal with women, not as the centerpiece of their life, however, as a device.

CHAPTER EIGHT

Flirting Skills that Comes Naturally to Women and Emotion

Teasing.

Women tease with their eyes, looking flirtatiously at guys, and then they move in so close in preventing their glance. They tease with the way they dress, using clothing that exposes so much, but not excessive.

Consider how strippers get you delighted and after that withdraw, get you thrilled, and then withdraw.

Women do this all the time, on a variety of levels. Because they recognize that foreplay begins long before you reach the bedroom, and women do it.

Tease a lady playfully, since she loves it. Tease her about :

- Her responses to your questions.

- The way she gowns.

- Her mannerisms and peculiarities.

Slap her in the ass when she says something bratty. Ball up a paper straw wrapper and toss it at her, with a mischievous smile on your face.

Frame the entire interaction with a woman practically like you're her big brother, and she's your humorous little sister. Keep everything lively and amusing.

Her Attraction Signals.

The reason is that if a female is staying speaking to you and being enjoyable, certainly she doesn't dislike you! But it's always possible that she likes you just as a friend (though unlikely as long as you keep pressing the interaction forward), so my advice is to learn and memorize the following list that I've developed, and after that, try to forget it.

The following list remains in no particular order.

1. She compliments you on almost anything.

2. She feels nervous around you. Look for indications of anxiousness, such as her muscle jerking.

3. She teases you playfully.

4. She makes an effort to inform you just how much she likes the same things you like.

5. She speaks about things that you both can do in the future. "You like vintage clothing stores too?" she may say, "We ought to go sometime!" By the way, this is likewise something you should raise with girls. Do not make it too major. (Say anything

playfully unreasonable that the two of you might carry out in the future. Keep it verbally non-sexual naturally.).

6. When her legs are crossed, look at the foot of her leading leg. It is an indication you've got her full attention if it is pointed toward you.

7. When it lulls, she makes an effort to keep the conversation going. Once in some time, you can even test her destination by purposely allowing the discussion to stop briefly on your end (See if she restarts the discussion.).

8. She touches her face. When an individual touches his or her face, it's a sign that they're thinking of something.

9. She gazes into your eyes and holds her gaze.

10. She stair at you. (Being passive by nature, women will follow the lead of a male they feel attracted to.)

- Adjusts the rate of her voice to match yours.

- Matches the pace of your breathing.

- Laughs together

11. Stroking around things such as a wine glass or pen up and down with her thumb and guideline finger. This suggests you have a strong result on her, good guy!

12. She tosses her head back or side-to-side. View her hair to sway as she does it.

13. She touches her face while taking a look at you.

14. She dangles her shoe off her foot or even takes it off.

15. She rubs her fingertips around her upper chest.

16. She rubs her palm on the back of her head, triggering her hair to fluff out.

17. She plays with her hair while looking at you.

18. She shows an authentic smile instead of one that's forced.

19. Because her pupils are big and dilated, her eyes sparkle.

20. She raises her eyebrows sometimes.

21. Her nipples are solidifying. Of course, you can only identify this if she's wearing the ideal clothing.

22. She has an unwinded face. (However, sometimes a non-relaxed face can be fine, such as when a female is so brought in to you that she feels nervous.).

23. She focuses all her attention on you, even when there are other individuals around.

24. She touches you while speaking to you, even if it is "accidental." Women are highly mindful of their bodies, so it will rarely indeed be an accident when they touch you. When she laughs at one of your witty statements, look for her to touch your arm to highlight a point or brush her foot versus yours.

25. She chuckles at your remarks as if they're the funniest things she's ever heard, even if they're just mildly amusing.

26. She reveals her tongue, like when she touches it to her front teeth or licks her lips.

27. With her body turned towards you, she unexpectedly sits upright, with her arm muscles tensed and her breasts pressed out.

28. She shows her palms to you. Open palms indicate she feels open with you.

29. She rubs her wrists or plays with her bracelet.

30. Her skin ends up being flushed. Look especially to observe whether she blushes. (This can also be a signal that she feels horny.).

31. She rubs her earlobes or plays with her earrings.

32. She asks you questions about yourself. They will not simply be the shallow questions that she 'd ask anyone (" Where are you from?"), however instead will be deeper questions to learn what makes you tick (e.g., "What are your enthusiasm in life?").

When a lady acts bratty and asks you some concern like, "Why did you decide to talk with me?" or "Do you say that things to all the ladies?" the very best thing to do is to not look for the most elegant response.

Instead, the best method to respond is with indifference. That method you remain in control of the frame. (Whenever you appreciate what a girl believes, that provides her the control.).

There's never a requirement to feel as if you need to captivate a female. Doing so makes you beta. Communicate with her when you converse with a woman. Screen her to be sure that she can keep a conversation opting for you. That makes you the alpha male.

As you constantly presume the female's brought in to you, the most crucial rule for keeping control of the frame us to always be ready to stroll away.

Although I discuss perseverance until you either get declined or laid, sometimes it's good to be the one to stroll away very first (if it's a girl you do not like), just to understand that you can. If a female views a guy as an obstacle, that keeps him compelling. It indicates she has to work for him, and if she acquires his affections, that's her benefit. Suppose you're ever a "sure" for a lady, that offers her validation and triggers her to lose destination for you. If you merely assume attraction, that ensures that the lady continually believes that she's more attracted to you than you are to her.

CHAPTER NINE

What Women Really Want from Men

The ancient question that has actually been asked by men all over the world is this:

What is it that women want from us?

To be honest with you, the answers are limitless. Since there are billions of women worldwide, they all may desire different things. Being the human that we are, there are certain things that both women and men desire that, for the most part, are non-negotiable.

These are the integrated needs that emerge from both our primal desires and our human nature. For that reason, it's important to frame the question of "what women want?" based upon a female's primal desires and requirements. Why? Well, it's because the answer will always be the same for each woman. Focusing our question on human nature and impulse will produce a bit more consistency in figuring out precisely what is that quality, a lady wants from a man.

So to simplify things a bit, the question that men need to ask is this:

What things do women want from men that can be thought about non-negotiable, universal, and primal?

Now that we have the RIGHT question, let me give you the RIGHT response:

The main point that a female desire from a man is the experience of feeling like a lady. She desires to lose herself in her womanhood, and the only method she can handle this feminine experience is when a man imitates as a guy.

Seriously, women are feminine creatures by nature and intuitively desire to be treated as such, no matter what society may state. It's the natural order of things, therefore the more feminine a lady probes a man, the more comfortable, secure, and desirable she will feel. It is this experience of feeling like a creature of feminine appeal that women these days are yearning for from men.

The lady of your dreams is yearning for the kind of man that can make her feel like a woman. And she has no option, however, to respond to the man that can activate this sensation within her.

This indicates that by establishing the sort of manly qualities of character that a female is Hard-Wired to respond to, you'll naturally make yourself alluring and irreplaceable to her.

The Masculine Character and Women

The more masculine a guy is, the more feminine he will make the women around him feel. And the term masculine, in this case, refers to a male's character and his habits. The best method for a male to develop a more manly disposition is to go about constructing his character and enhancing his character purposely.

Simply put, as a man, you need to take control of your life, take duty for your ideas and actions, and find out to handle your emotions effectively.

If you wish to impress a female, or rather, the perfect kind of high-quality lady that you wish to bring in, the very first thing you need to do is concentrate on building your character and making yourself far more masculine in a natural sense.

This is the only crucial thing you can do in this life. Nothing is more appealing to a quality woman than a man who places a high worth on things like sincerity and integrity, and other qualities of a sterling, noble character. And while physical strength does count for a lot in stimulating a female's physical attraction, keeping her drawn in over the long-term means that a guy should also have the strength- of character.

A lady wishes to know that she can be sure of her experience with you. She would like to see that she can depend upon you while times are excellent. She desires to be confident in your ability to handle temptation if you're faced with the chance to do something questionable to acquire something you desire. In these circumstances, she wishes to be sure of your stability, as she hopes that you won't do something that doesn't align with your beliefs just to earn a profit or enjoy a minute of fleeting enjoyment.

This is VERY crucial to her.

On the other hand, a woman likewise wishes to know that she can rely on you to deal with disputes when times aren't so good. She wants to be guaranteed that she's with a MAN through and through. When things are going well and then fall apart at the joints when a dispute arises, she does not want to feel as if you might just be simple. You'll wind up looking like an inexperienced little boy, and trust me, that won't be a fun experience for either of you.

A woman would like to know that you can make her feel preferable, safe, and secure, womanly, and gorgeous. She would like to know that you're the type of man she can grow with, one who can help her grow and reach her complete capacity as a female. And the more masculine you remain in character, the simpler it will be to make her feel in this manner naturally.

And when it pertains to the romance department, the manly man is a heroic and irresistible fan to his female. He knows how to meet her both physically and emotionally, and he makes it his responsibility to ensure that her deepest needs for physical and psychological intimacies are regularly fulfilled.

How to Build a Powerful Masculine Character.

Character building for a male is maybe the most important task he might ever carry out in his life. I know it was and still is, for me at least.

As soon as I began to concentrate on changing certain aspects of my character, I started to see the outcomes in my life change too. And think it or not, the sort of life you lead and the sort of woman you'll draw in and keep will all depend upon who you are as a male.

All of your lead to life will be based on who you are at your masculine core. Your train of idea, your automatic responses to situations, and how you handle disputes and other individuals are all connected to your character. Women are much more attracted to a guy's character and character than by his appearances, accomplishments, or belongings. Much more so, premium, smart women, those with more experience in handling men, tend to have a fundamental ability to see a guy for what he truly is on the within, regardless of the halo effect created by his physical look or the material representations of his high-status.

Fortified with this understanding, it is of best interest for you to focus on the advancement of your character and personality.

This is just a beginning point, however for the sake of helping you to get your feet wet, here are a few manly character-building tips:

1. Start a brand-new severe pastime, something that you can see yourself ending up being truly great at. This will build your strong self-confidence, and it will also assist you in establishing discipline as you develop your ability and increase your knowledge in a brand-new way.

2. Develop a brand-new ability or an old skill and use it as a method to get ahead in your career or perhaps build a service. This will assist you in taking conscious control of the self-development procedure by forcing you to hone your psychological faculties to be imaginative in your work.

3. Travel with your woman frequently and strategize extraordinary experiences with her. Take the effort and make it your company to guarantee that her life is filled with romantic fun and adventure.

4. Set a challenging goal for yourself and devote yourself to attaining it. This will help you to build character and will reveal your female that you are goal-driven and enthusiastic.

5. Sign up with a health club or sports team or get a martial art and develop your body. This is critically important.

Why? Since physical strength and martial guts are two qualities that have been considered absolutely "masculine," in its purest essence, throughout human history. And although it may not look like it, establishing your physical strength and increasing your capacity for martial nerve also assists your character development. Pursuing such activities will increase your male confidence while at the very same time, making you much more physically attractive to women on a biological and primal level. It will also assist you in developing self-discipline and proficiency, as ending up being skilled in any kind of weightlifting, sports, or martial arts will require fantastic amounts of effort and persistence.

6. Find out more books that will propel you forward in life. Any book that will help in your advancement (like this one) will help you to construct a more compelling character by sharpening your psychological faculties and your ability to fix problems.

7. Discover some buddies that will assist you to stand out in life. Sign up with a social club where men collect and find methods to

include worth to the gathering and your community. This will assist you in growing in character as you are forced to learn how to relate much better with other men to get your requirements fulfilled and the needs of others by working together.

8. Come up with fun and creative methods to reveal your affection on an on-going basis. This will assist you in establishing the virtues of love and appreciation, as the more you pour yourself into the relationship, the higher benefits you will enjoy.

9. Be proactive. Offer up recommendations to resolve disputes, be the very first one to make a move, and take more initiative. Discover to end up being a skillful decision-maker. This will assist you in developing the skillful quality of personal initiative.

10. Go above and beyond the call of responsibility in your love life and establish your manly resourcefulness in your relationship. Discover what makes your female tick and ensure that her requirements are satisfied even before she recognizes she had one. This will help you to establish the habit of going the extra mile and over- providing on your pledges and commitments.

Those ideas ought to be sufficient to help get you started.

Even though they're all pretty helpful suggestions, you've got to do the work. Start with something and commit to seeing it through. Do something about it now, and obstacle yourself. This is the only way to construct the strong character that you desire and the manly qualities that the female of your dreams will require in order to submit to your management. Keep in mind, cultivating a strong, manly character is essential for any male who desires higher success and relationship happiness.

Basing our inquiry on human nature and impulse will bring about a bit more consistency in figuring out precisely what it is that a quality woman wants from and in a man.

The Key to Her Heart: Earning and Keeping Trust
A woman can just love and respect you as a male as far as she can rely on being with you. It's as simple as that, my friend. Above all else, she needs security from you.

This is why women have the habit of testing men, day in and day out. It is a subconscious practice that is constructed into their mind. When it comes to earning and keeping her trust, since of this requirement for certainty, a woman will continue to check a man throughout his life to ensure that she can rely on him during the bad times and even the excellent times.

Now, you must keep in mind that these tests aren't truly indicated to trigger any unwanted tension or to bring drama in your life. They are implied to keep you on your toes and to "persuade" you into being a better male or at least into being a guy, duration. For a woman, testing you will reveal to her the difference between who you state you are and what you're made from.

Checking you enables her unfiltered access to the true nature of your character, as she assesses the places in which you lack congruence.

Initially, it might be simple for you to get by on a charming personality alone. Under a wise woman's testing, any façade you may be attempting to present to her will not hold up over time. You can be as charming and as dashing as you desire, but in the long-run, your real character will expose itself. More experienced women are familiar with this, and they'll keep testing you until the "real," authentic you finally presents himself.

Her Experience with You

What a woman wishes to be sure of more than anything is her experience with you. This exceeds her physical senses in that she desires to feel secure with you in mind, body, and soul. When the going gets tough, she wants to know how you'll deal with her psychological nature, and she wants to know if she can rely on you.

What she truly wants is a feeling of security, knowing that no matter what life throws her way, you'll exist as a source of strength and encouragement. She desires to feel safe in your capability to weather the storms of life.

The factor for this is because a lady is naturally hardwired to seek out power and security from a male to endure, as ending up with a weak, fluctuating, or predatory man can significantly endanger her presence.

This is why an intelligent, top quality lady will not only be extremely brought in to a male with a strong character; however, she'll end up being extremely bought a man who has ambition and drive. Without this certainty, a lady will not be brought in to you, or if she discovers that you're incapable of making her feel safe and secure over the long-lasting, she can not stay drawn into you.

CHAPTER TEN

The Secrets of Being an Irresistible Catch

The trick to acquiring and maintaining the love, admiration, regard, and desire of a quality woman is to progress into a much better male continually. As an intellectual man, you must never stop growing. You should never stop developing knowingly. As a guy, you ought to always be seeking the next level, a much better paradigm, and a more excellent perfect as you live your life.

I might probably sum up this entire book with this one concept: Women are brought in to men who illustrate the characteristics and qualities of leadership. An excellent woman will stick to a trustworthy man and follow his path of leadership. Her love, regard, and desire for him will continue to grow so long as he can captivate her mind, body, and soul by making her an irreplaceable partner in his grand adventure.

An excellent female desire a guy who can lead her, one who can make the hard decisions. She desires a man that can gain her self-confidence, and she desires him to take her for who she is and to love her deeply and romantically.

To keep her mesmerized, you need to progress. Your dedication to on-going personal development will mesmerize and amaze her continually. Your desire to enhance yourself alone is a turn-on for her merely because women are designed to be our indispensable equivalents.

What does it take to establish a fully grown character that will captivate an excellent female for life?

What does it require to have that masculine sensation of power that just comes when a guy takes obligation for his life and pursues his own course?

Let's dive in and discover out, shall we?

- Take Responsibility for Your Life

People don't provide you responsibilities when you're a guy. Even if they are "required" upon you, you will not have the ability to carry out at your greatest up until you "take" it upon yourself.

Leaders take responsibilities; they do not wait on it to be offered to them. Taking responsibility is the first and most crucial to consider as a man's development if he wishes to rid himself of the whiny little young boy inside of him. A guy must discover to avoid blaming individuals and situations for his results and must take full responsibility for his whole life instead.

Learn to take ownership of the choices you've made. Accept the truth that you are where you are in life since of the decisions that you've made, which the outcome of your tomorrow will be based on the choices you make today.

If your personality attracted her, but you still maintain the boylike attitude of blame and playing the victim, she'll quickly find herself losing her desire for you.

- This is a slow and agonizing death.

To take duty in your life, very first accept whatever the way it is. No matter what your life looks like, just accept it as the outcome of your choices and begin planning ways to improve it. This will bring you much assurance and a much better sense of control over the future results in your life.

- Discover Your Path and Never Stray from It

A male without a clear course in life is merely wandering through the world aimlessly and with no direction. No excellent woman in her right mind is going to desire to come along for that ride, a minimum of not for long.

Understanding your purpose and following your distinct path in life will provide you a deep sense of what it suggests to be devoted to something larger than yourself. It will give you an inner voice and belonging that will encourage you to make favorable modifications worldwide around you.

It will become your fixation, your mission in life to fulfill this purpose. You will live a much happier and successful experience as soon as you've found your purpose and choose to stick to your course, no matter what.

Having this special course will make you a lot more effective in the world and a lot more attractive to the right woman who can assist you in the accomplishment of your life's goals.

As long as you make your mission the essential element of your life, you'll never have to worry about losing the desire of the right lady merely because she will end up being extremely interested and invested in you attaining what you set your heart on.

And as soon as you know what your function in life is, you'll discover that it is easier to have peace of mind when things do not constantly go as you've planned.

Naturally, discovering your path may require some deal with your part. It will take some effort in self-reflection and some soul browsing. Trust me, it is worth it in the long-run.

- Quit Consuming and Become a Producer

No, this has absolutely nothing to do with films, music, or end up being the next Rick Rubin or Quincy Jones. This has to do with ending up being an incredibly productive creator, contractor, and company in your family, community, and your piece of the world. One of the key things that separate the mature man leader from the average Joe is that one is a manufacturer, and the other is a consumer.

The average Joe takes in more than he offers to the world in terms of worth, but leaders provide more than they get in terms of worth. The manufacturer will always be greater than the consumer. Absolutely nothing is more evident in the lives of fantastic men than the reality that they were men who found out how to develop and offer huge amounts of worth in their communities. They used their imaginative resources to build, pioneer, construct, and produce new and important things.

If you wish to grow and reach your greatest capacities on your own, your lady, and your neighborhood, you should end up being a prolific manufacturer. The path to male management needs that a guy abandoned his childish methods of believing to establish a mindset of prolific imagination.

Through the efficient management of your time, cash, and resources, you can improve your levels of efficiency and imagination to add more value to the world than what you draw from it.

- Master Your Fears

Two main fears can obstruct a man from achieving success in not just his relationships, however, in any area of his life. These two things are the fear of failure and the worry of criticism.

A leader discovers to overcome these fears by mastering his feelings. He understands that failure is simply a step on the course to attainment, and that criticism is simply a sign that he is alive and doing something rewarding and productive with his life.

You can not prosper in any way if you can not fail forward. And if you do not discover how to handle criticism, then you will not be able to do anything that matters to anybody.

To master your worries, you must master your feelings. You can do this by changing your concept about failure itself.

- Failure is rarely irreversible.

Instead, see it as a stepping stone and a lesson found out. See it as something you MUST go through to accomplish success.

When it comes to criticism, if it's positive, simply see it as a method to enhance what you're doing. If you're too attached to what you're doing, unfavorable criticism can only harm you.

Instead, find out to love the procedure of becoming instead of being solely concentrated on the result. If you can do this, you'll hardly ever need to worry about criticism from others.

A leader does not need the approval of others, consisting of women. However, if he's in a healthy relationship with the best lady, he will seek her counsel when the time calls for it. However, otherwise, he is self- approved most importantly, and this displays in the clearness of his thinking and the powerful outcomes of his decisions.

Mastering your fears will end up being more comfortable as you end up being a much better male. As you grow into a complete understanding of who you are and what you're capable of, you'll have a greater comfort when dealing with the lots of unknowns in your life.

As a guy, you need always to be seeking the next level, a much better paradigm, and a greater ideal as you live your life.

A good lady will choose to follow and trust a man who is knowingly following the course of leadership. A male must find out to prevent blaming people and circumstances for his outcomes and ought to rather take complete obligation for his whole life.

Ask several men you know what their path in life is, and most of them most likely can't provide you a concise and clear answer. A male without a clear course in life is just wandering through the world aimlessly and without any instructions.

- Cultivate Masculine Courage

I can provide you no much better guidance for attaining success in your relationship with your lady and other areas of your life than this:

Challenge yourself purposely and regularly every day of your life. This will construct the most important particular found in ALL excellent leaders and highly successful people of society. It will develop your guts.

We've most likely covered this a lot of times already; however, it can not be stated enough. A guy's courage to do what is right, to follow his course in life, to defend what he believes in, and to be the very best variation of himself is his most preferable and appealing quality to a female.

Courage can only be cultivated by purposely doing it. Courage is something you "DO" It's not something you believe about. It's an action you TAKE. A guy can develop systems of his guts by doing the essential things he's typically averse to doing.

I think that self-confidence is merely the way we communicate our levels of guts to others. It's impossible to have one without the other. Intellectual and physical courage is incredibly important; it is ethical courage that is especially important to a female.

Ethical courage will provide you the strength and ability to exercise all of your other virtues. It will assist you in making the best decision no matter what others may think about you. This is among the most necessary elements that separate the typical man from the man who leads others.

The guy with terrific quantities of courage is not scared to state what needs to be said and to do what should be done. And any lady would be more than ready to put her confidence and rely on such a guy.

- Accept Yourself Now

It's fantastic how I'm about to cover everything up with this last piece of suggestions viewing as though your mission is to become a better male for the lady who's right for you. It may appear inconsistent, but believe me, it isn't.

You MUST discover how to accept yourself for who you are and for where you remain in life beginning today. Although your mission as a mature man is to develop and reach your greatest capacity continuously, if you fail to accept yourself and discover contentment in your present phase of development, you will not be reliable in becoming the best version of yourself.

All change begins with self-acceptance. You should discover to acknowledge your present value in the present state you're in because if you do not, you'll continuously prevent yourself whenever you disappoint your development objectives and individual vision.

Forgive yourself magnanimously every single day. Provide yourself a break for Pete's sake and decline to berate yourself for any factor whatsoever.

Stop stressing over what other men are doing and remain concentrated on what is right for you at your phase of development and advancement. Become a master at self-acceptance by being grateful for what you have.

Master the art of revealing gratitude in your everyday life, and your life will change drastically.

Here's a life-changing suggestion: if you don't take anything else from this book (which I doubt), and this is the only thing that you find out, you WILL delight in better relationships in every area of your life:

Cultivate the practice of being grateful for your life just as it is today, and how you 'd like it to be in the future. Make it a HABIT to see the favorable side of things, and develop a positive personality towards life. Program your gratitude in how you live your life and EXPECT good ideas to occur to you.

And yes, it is possible to turn into a more positive and capable guy while being content with who you are right now. Just concentrate on your strengths and the important things you like about yourself.

All it takes is a determination always to pursue the very best, balanced with the decision always to forgive yourself rapidly whenever you do fail.

A great female does not desire an ideal man per se; she simply wants a guy who's ideal for her. The simple truth that you've devoted yourself to her and a path of constant personal development is all that she needs to appreciate, regard, and remain in love with you for as long as you want.

- Continuously Seek Wisdom

I 'd much like to end our talk with one final piece of advice:

Don't be afraid to get great guidance that can help you to enhance yourself and your relationships.

Now, if you've read this book, then you undoubtedly don't have that problem, but this is just a pointer. Too frequently, we decide to follow a particular path thinking that we've got it all found out or that we'll simply "go with the flow."

Although going with the flow can be enjoyable, there's nothing more encouraging than knowing your side as your guide. It's better to be prepared in any situation, no matter how much you think you might already know.

Good ideas just began to change in my love life when I started to seek out excellent guidance and use it. Some of it was free, some of it I paid for, but in the end, it was all worth it.

As men, we can be a bit stubborn and prideful, especially when it concerns getting this location of our lives dealt with. Nevertheless, when a male decides to arm himself with a bit (or a lot) of knowledge, a whole new world of possibilities begins to open up for him.

When it concerns his relationship with his perfect lady, the more he educates himself, the better he ends up being to her.

So remember to keep knowing and to continue your advancement path towards developing as a man. It'll make your romantic life much richer and more satisfying in the long-run. Do this, and the best lady will see you as a tempting catch, the sort of male that she 'd rather not live her life without.

CONCLUSION

Before you go, I 'd like to state "thank you" for getting my book. I understand you could have selected from dozens of books on comprehending women; however, you bet on my guide, and for that, I'm exceptionally grateful. Thanks again for checking out all the method to the end.

A man can build systems of his nerve by doing the things he's generally averse to doing. Physical and intellectual guts are essential; it is ethical guts that are especially important to a woman. This is one of the most vital aspects that separate the typical male from the male who leads others.

Remember to keep on knowing and to continue on your advancement path towards maturing as a male. Do this the perfect woman will see you as an irresistible catch, the kind of male that she 'd rather not live her life without.